Tiempos Lejanos

Mary Burritt Christiansen Poetry Series
Vincent Barrett Price, Series Editor

Also available in the University of New Mexico Press
Mary Burritt Christiansen Poetry Series

Miracles of Sainted Earth
Victoria Edwards Tester

Poets of the Non-Existent City
Edited by Estelle Gershgoren Novak

Amulet Songs, Lucille Adler

Selected Poems of Gabriela Mistral
Translated by Ursula K. Le Guin

Deeply Dug In, R. L. Barth

In Company
Edited by Lee Bartlett, V. B. Price,
and Dianne Edenfield Edwards

Mary Burritt
Christiansen
Poetry Series

TIEMPOS LEJANOS

Poetic Images from the Past

NASARIO GARCÍA

Translated from the Spanish by the Author

UNIVERSITY OF NEW MEXICO PRESS
ALBUQUERQUE

First paperbound printing, 2005
Paperbound ISBN 0-8263-3301-X

09 08 07 06 05 1 2 3 4 5

Library of Congress Cataloging-in-Publication Data

García, Nasario.
Tiempos lejanos : poetic images from the past / Nasario García.— 1st ed.
p. cm. — (Mary Burritt Christiansen poetry series)
Spanish with English translations.
ISBN 0-8263-3300-1 (cloth : alk. paper)
1. García, Nasario—Translations into English.
2. New Mexico—Poetry. I. Title. II. Series.
PQ7079.2.G35A2 2004
861'.64—dc22

2004015438

Design and composition: Mina Yamashita

Facing page: Photo by Nasario García, the author's parents near Laguna de don Ricardo south of Cabezón Peak, 1948.
Page 1: Photo courtesy of the author,
La Matanza, c. 1922–24, Guadalupe, NM.
Nasario P. García, the author's father, is 2nd from left.

A mis queridos padres.
A quienes echo mucho de menos.
Q. D. E. P.

† Nasario P. García
†Agapita López-García

EL SILENCIO

OYE, *hijo mío, el silencio.*
Es un silencio ondulado,
un silencio,
donde resbalan valles y ecos
y que inclina las frentes
hacia el suelo

—FEDERICO GARCÍA LORCA

De un mundo callado
se estremecen
y estallan
estas palabras
de mi pasado.

Como viejo zapato
en su horma,
buen corazón
con pocas palabras
se conforma.

—El Autor

From a silent world
spring these words
from my past
that tremble first
and then explode.

Like an old shoe
in its last,
a kind heart
is content with
just a few words.

—The Author

Contents

FOREWORD

Certain parts of the planet, that might be called "places of power," seem more graced with spiritual and physical beauty than others. And the Rio Puerco Valley, northwest of Albuquerque, New Mexico, is one of those places. Poet and scholar Nasario García writes of the majestic solitude of that landscape, and the strength and gentility of spirit it inspired in the people who worked its land and weathered its hardships.

In his lucidly clear and emotionally intense first book of poems, *Tiempos lejanos*, Dr. García, the distinguished New Mexico folklorist, writes through the experience of his childhood in the 1940s. The poems focus on a long silenced world lived around a small agricultural community, abandoned by the late 1950s, called Ojo Del Padre, or Guadalupe today.

Written in Spanish and translated into English by the author, *Tiempos lejanos—Poetic Images from the Past,* uncovers for its readers a way of life that remains an icon of hardiness, family solidarity, profound faith, and a clear headed, disciplined patience working the land. The landscape of the Rio Puerco Valley, cut through by what might be called in English Muddy River, is dominated by the greatest number of volcanic necks, or plugs, in close proximity anywhere in the world. The largest, El Cabezon, or The Big Head, "father of the giants," in Dr. García's words, towers over the valley by almost 2,000 feet and can be seen from as far as way as the northeast end of the Sandia Mountains more than 70 miles distant. All across the valley other plugs sprout up from desert floor, some of which Dr. García names in one poem—Twin Peaks, Mares' Peak, Billy Goat Peak, Hog's Peak. Such names remind us that wherever people are, they anchor themselves to the landscape through the ownership bestowed by naming.

These poems of place ring so deeply true to people who love the land, and who have worked the land, however marginally, that they well up inside one a nostalgia for places and things in one's life that beckon with a silence of their own. García's poem "The Hoe" connects all readers who've hoed their garden patch, hand file in their back pockets waiting to sharpen the blade so it can nick out that final weed around the tomatoes. But in García's poem, the hoe takes on further qualities, ones known, perhaps, only to people who've worked the land in isolation and staunch self-reliance: "With his hoe/he hoes,/he digs,/ he irrigates, mixes mud./ With his hoe/he defends/ his homing instinct/and his honor./With his hoe/he chops off the heads/of snakes/ that slither/on the ground/or walk on foot."

Just as it would be impossible to comprehend the life and times of Ojo del Padre by spending only a day there in its prime, so too it would be a disservice to each of the poems in *Tiempos lejanos* to treat them only as separate entities. Each one is connected to the ones before and after it, and each plays its part in conveying how life was lived, and how the meaning of the days and years was interpreted by the lives that cooperated to survive in the dry lands and unpredictable weather of Ojo del Padre.

This is a book to be read whole. Without a complete reading, Ojo del Padre remains a ghost town, much like it was when I ventured there some 42 years ago in an old truck on what seemed to me then as a wild adventure into the roadless outback west of Albuquerque. With a whole reading of *Tiempos lejanos*, the town comes alive, as it might in the first blush of imagination on seeing its ruins. Crossing the dry Rio Puerco that year, I came across the old adobe church with its huge wood cross in the court yard. Up the rise from the river was an amazing sight, a two-story wooden dance hall, and a few smaller commercial buildings, and the ruins of homes. It was hard that day not to project an entire emotional history on that town fed by my imagination alone. It was wonderful then, and now with Nasario García's disarmingly clear and startling direct poems, the life and the world of a place lost in its abandonment comes truly back to life, as if the reader had just walked into a home at supper time and smelled onions, chile, pork, and masa simmering on the wood stove.

Professor García re-teaches a potent lesson with these poems. Every place in the world is the center of the universe for those who live there, and only those who do live there can know its secret heart, its core, its bold yearnings, ennobling griefs, and redeeming joys.

Dr. García's career has for years given readers a sense of what Hispanic New Mexico was in the early and middle years of the 20th century. As a professor emeritus of languages, a former Dean of the College of Arts and Sciences at New Mexico Highlands University in Las Vegas, and a tireless scholar, Nasario García's bibliography is too full to cover completely. Recent work includes *Más antes: Hispanic Folklore of the Río Puerco Valley*; *Comadres: Hispanic Women of the Río Puerco Valley*, which he edited; *Brujas, Bultos, y Brasas: Tales of Witchcraft and the Supernatural in the Río Pecos Valley*; *Plácitas: Conversations with Hispano Writers of*

New Mexico; and most recently *Chistes: Hispanic Humor of Northern New Mexico and Southern Colorado*

.

Mary Burrit Christiansen, the poet who endowed UNM Press's poetry series, wrote often about solitude and silence. I am sure *Tiempos lejanos—Poetic Images from the Past* would moved her deeply, as it has moved me, with a sense of camaraderie and inner recognition.

—V.B. Price
Albuquerque, June 2004

PREFACE

Time slips away from the poet as from everyone else. For the poet, however, the eternal movement from past to future, with its illusion of a "present" that eludes any attempt to grasp and hold it, offers a unique opportunity. Nasario García fully understands poetry as a vision of the past—not a historical or a sociological interpretation of the past, but an aesthetic picture of it. Poetry does not necessarily offer religious assurances about the past. Nor does it offer an interpretation, as philosophy or history might advance. Rather, poetry is close to Ludwig (Josef Johann) Wittgenstein's insight of the use of language, of sentences, to convey pictures of the world. For Nasario García, as for many poets, poetry is a personal "picture," or series of pictures, about the past. In this particular collection, the past is the immediate past and it is specific as to place.

Tiempos lejanos recalls the village of Ojo del Padre, now called Guadalupe, New Mexico. The poems take us back to the late forties and early fifties of the last century, when rural towns in New Mexico were about to leap from the pre-industrial era into the post-industrial world, with all the concomitant constructive and destructive forces that such change would unleash.

For the reader unfamiliar with New Mexico or the Southwest, it might be well to recall that the common view of America being settled by hunters, trappers, merchants, pioneers, and settlers, in a movement from east to west, is false and disturbing. It is false because for over two centuries before the inexorable westward push of Anglos from the East Coast to the West Coast of North America, there was a Hispanic thrust from south to north, from Mexico City north to Chihuahua, El Paso del Norte, and on to Santa Fe and the southern reaches of Colorado. Other branches of this Hispanic exploration, colonization and migration reached north to Texas, Arizona, and California. The idea of an east-to-west primary pattern of settlement is disturbing because it distorts the past, obscures the multicultural reality of the Southwest, and handicaps Americans with a deep ignorance of how this land was forged by people of many different cultures and languages.

Once the reader is armed with this knowledge, it becomes understandable that a community such as Ojo del Padre, even though it is geographically located in the American Southwest, has a character formed by nearly four hundred years of Hispanic presence. And for most of those four hundred years, Ojo del Padre, and many villages like it, nurtured the Spanish language, as well as the customs and traditions of Spain and Mexico, passed down from generation to generation, and the strong family and communal bonds that made it possible to survive in a beautiful but harsh and demanding environment.

Nasario García explores the rich world of Ojo del Padre from the point of view of a boy who grew up there. He captures the landscape, the village and its people, the birds and animals both domestic and wild, of this domain at the moment when they shine with the dying brilliance of the setting sun, just before they are extinguished forever.

There is a deceptive simplicity to these poems. At their most accessible level, the narrative poems explore the world of Ojo del Padre in minute detail. It would be false, however, to distinguish too sharply between the narrative and lyrical poems here because there is a strong lyrical quality in all of them.

At a deeper level, Nasario García has written these poems with a fine sense of craft. He maintains the point of view of a child throughout this collection, yet he varies the *rima asonante*, assonant vowel rhyme, in many subtle ways. He makes use of variable stanzaic structures and patterns and he uses many poetic devices such as repetition of lines and sounds, dialogue, alliteration, and iambic and trochaic substitutions. There is rich humor, in the midst of personal loss and cultural tragedy, running through these poems. In them, there is the confluence of the powerful sense of nature with the intimacy of detail about the daily life of Ojo del Padre as seen principally but not exclusively in the family experiences of the young observer-poet who expresses himself through striking metaphors.

Spanish distinguishes between *lengua*, or the language one speaks, and *lenguaje*, or the manner in which a person or a community speaks and writes. These poems link the ancient Spanish literary forms, the *jarchas* of the tenth and eleventh centuries, with the specific *lenguaje*, the manner in which the villagers of Ojo del Padre express themselves. The result is that the archaic elements of Spanish have combined with certain Anglicisms and indigenous, mainly Náhuatl, expressions, to produce a profoundly authentic New Mexican rural Spanish. These poems are written in a language Miguel de Cervantes would have recognized and enjoyed, the language that was familiar to Francisco Quevedo, and the language with which the mystic poets of Spain and Mexico would have felt at ease. This is no small accomplishment for a poet who has restricted his range to a poetic memoir about one time and place as seen from the young narrator's perspective.

Tiempos lejanos, in the poet's own words, "reflects, above all, a personal past that is as much real as it is lyrical." These poems are "pictures," as it were, of this past, but they are not still shots. Their lyrical dynamism, created by the poet, carries them over from the past into the passing moment and beyond to the indefinite future. At least for this moment we have this stunning evocation in authentic Spanish of an all but vanished way of life in New Mexico.

Nasario García introduces his poems with a brief epigraph from Federico García Lorca that speaks of the epeirogenic nature of the world, the undulating silence of it, a silence into which valleys and echoes fall away and which makes us bow our heads towards the ground. There is another concept Lorca uses which is quite appropriate for these poems. That is the concept of *duende*, the spirit that sparks the imagination into powerful, explosive, creation. These poems have *duende* and they make us lift our heads to salute the remote times of Ojo del Padre. With these poems, the village and its time in history are recreated for the living and for those who will come after us.

—E. A. "TONY" MARES
Albuquerque, March 12, 2002

INTRODUCTION

Ojo del Padre (Guadalupe in more modern times) is the little village (*placita*) where I grew up in the Río Puerco Valley some forty-five miles northwest of Albuquerque. Like many Hispanic communities of northern New Mexico, it had its church, oratory, school, dance hall, post office, and grocery store, with a population that scarcely reached 50 inhabitants when I was a small boy. Today Ojo del Padre lies in ruins, not only testimony to a glorious past, but also a victim of the dreams and hopes of a poor yet proud people who were forced to escape to Albuquerque and its environs in search of a better life. Although they abandoned their village or their homes nearby along the confluence of the Río Puerco, my own parents among them, what people never did was to toss their reminiscences over their shoulders and thus forget about life in the countryside. Nor have I, because my upbringing in rural New Mexico represents the formative years of my life.

Tiempos lejanos—Poetic Images from the Past comprises poems that attempt to capture the spirit of my childhood as seen through my own eyes while growing up in Ojo del Padre. I envisioned a universe that went —and which often times took me—beyond the confines of my daily realities. It was my way of viewing life on the one hand, and a means of entertaining myself, on the other, in an environment where no television, radio, or even books in which I could immerse myself existed, all of which enabled me to retreat from my own daily existence into a world of reverie and curiosity. I was fascinated by rural life in the desert where the landscape, the sky, the animals, the birds, and the people brought both happiness and sorrow to my heart, but at the same time each one inveigled my imagination.

I will never forget my youthful exploits on horseback, galloping at times fearlessly through ravines replete with prairie dog mounds—dodging the playful critters—feeling a sense of invulnerability. Seeing the arroyos and their watering places (*aguajes*) bubble with foam following the summer thunderstorms, or the remaining seasons that changed character according to their climatic conditions or temperament, likewise added to my repertoire of remembrances. Nor can I ever take lightly my wonderful memories of the majestic volcanic plugs and hills that dominated the scenery, or the Río Puerco, a fascinating, mysterious, and even mystical river whose violent and sweeping waters left me mesmerized, but which from one day to the next could also run with such tranquility so as to leave you in a somnambulistic state.

Tiempos lejanos reflects, above all, a personal past that is as much real as it is lyrical. The words and sounds in this mélange of poems consist of the poetics of my own being lodged in a world in which my parents raised me. Their way of life, coupled with the customs and traditions and the Spanish language (my native tongue) they taught me, mirror what I have tried to express in the ensuing poems. Whether it is pain, happiness, humor, love, violence, humility, respect, compassion or neglect, they all attest to a kaleidoscope of emotions offered here in Spanish and English.

The English version of this dichotomous yet conjoined world of poetry and passion merits a brief explanation. The translation of literary works is an imperfect science at best. Rarely does a translation uphold the integrity of a work in its original language; this reality is especially true when a literary work involves poetry. Poetic ingredients such as structure and rhythm inevitably are diluted or even lost in a language different from the original. Metaphors, similes, and poetic imagery may suffer a similar fate as well.

Furthermore, language and culture are inseparable; one cannot exist without the other. Culturally charged terms in Spanish such as *resolana*, *hijito*, and *respeto* encountered in my repertoire of poems, as well as idiomatic expressions (e.g., *hinchársele a uno el cuajo*), possess their own individuality and *raison d'être* and hence pose a special challenge to the translator. To render a transliteration of *hijito* as "little son" as though it were simply a diminutive of "hijo" (son), or *respeto* for respect in a straightforward and simplistic fashion, ignoring or unaware of its underyling cultural implications, can often be misleading and inadequate. At times it is necessary to read more than just between the lines; one must read between words or even syllables to grasp the true essence of what lies beneath a word or an expression.

The impact of terms such as those mentioned above oftentimes is felt and experienced intuitively within one's cultural milieu and thus requires (or required) no explanation to children or grandchildren from parents or grandparents regarding their inherent cultural significance. Of equal importance, too, is the fact that many words found braided—arm in arm—in *Tiempos lejanos* are either dying or no longer exist even among old-timers reared in rural New Mexico. And with the demise of these and other terms, the power of language and culture is diminished and in due time silenced into oblivion. As Stephen King aptly put it: "What's lost has a way of staying lost."

The English rendition of *Tiempos lejanos* may not always convey the true poetic thrust of the respective poems compared to the Spanish, but it is hoped that their essence and spirit come across in a lucid and somewhat lyrical form for the monolingual English reader to enjoy. Each poem is an image, a cultural snapshot, as it were, of the world I knew, lived, and felt. The manner in which I perceived this seemingly vast yet circumscribed universe of mine while growing up in my native village of Ojo del Padre in the Río Puerco Valley of New Mexico is what I hereby offer the benevolent reader.

—Nasario Garcia
Santa Fe, New Mexico, 2004

Tiempos Lejanos

Remote Times

TIEMPOS LEJANOS

Tiempos lejanos
quedan reguardados
en un rincón
traicionero de
mi memoria
que se desesperan
por escaparse
para gozar de
la libertad y
del bien estar
de mi desierto
donde hoy día
todo está muerto.

REMOTE TIMES

Remote times
embedded in the past
remain well guarded
in a precarious
quoin
of my memory
yearning
to escape
so as to enjoy
the freedom
and well being
of my desert
where today
every thing is silent.

MI CABALLO BAYO

Vengo andando a pie
del Ojo Esquipula
donde se ve una mula

sin mi caballo bayo.

Pastó quelite
del burro
con un susurro
y tragó agua salitre

mi caballo bayo.

Le dio un torzón
luego un desazón

a mi caballo bayo.

Más lelo que muerto
con un ojo tuerto,
corta su vista mide,
se me despide

mi caballo bayo.

Me cuelgo al seno
las riendas del freno,
trabo en mi cabecilla
los estribos de la silla

de mi caballo bayo.

Atravieso El Aguaje
con mucho coraje,
bajo por La Cañada Ancha
caliente como una plancha

sin mi caballo bayo.

MY BAY HORSE

I'm headed back afoot
from Ojo de Esquipula
where I spot a mule

without my bay horse.

He ate silver-like
poisonous spinach
in secret and drank
saltpeter water

my bay horse did.

He suffered uneasiness
then a discomfort

my bay horse did.

More dazed than dead
with one eye shut,
his sight in short demand,
he bids me farewell

my bay horse does.

I drape the bridle's
reins around my chest
and fasten the stirrups
to the saddle horn

belonging to my bay horse.

I cross *El Aguaje*
in a state of anger
and go down
La Cañada Ancha
where it's hotter than blazes

without my bay horse.

Voy viendo en la loma
a mi mamá que se asoma
por la ventana de la cocina,
que queda en la mera esquina,
contando los pasos lentos
que voy dando violentos

sin mi caballo bayo.

Llego con el subadero
en la tierra arrastrando
por la cara derramando
lágrimas amargas de suero
que se resbalan sin aliento
por cada látigo y tiento

sin mi caballo bayo.

Sale mamá de la cocina,
aquella cara tan fina,
me da un cariñoso abrazo,
pues ya adivina el caso
en su ansioso pecho
mi doloroso despecho

sin mi caballo bayo.

I begin to discern atop the hill
my Mom peeking her head
out the kitchen window
from a corner of the house,
counting the slow steps
I take as I stomp the ground

minus my bay horse.

I reach home,
saddle blanket
dragging on the dirt,
as bitter tears of whey drip
and roll down my face
as they cascade breathlessly
down each leather strap

minus my bay horse.

Out comes my Mom
from the kitchen
wearing that delicate face of hers
and gives me an affectionate hug,
for her anxious heart
and grieving pain know
the whole story concerning me

minus my bay horse.

¿YA VOTÓ COMPADRE?

—¿Ya votó compadre?

—Pos sí. ¡Cómo que no!

—¿Y cuántas veces votó?

—Pos dos.

—¿Y cómo l'hizo?

—Pos me dieron dos votos.

—¿Dos qué?

—¡Dos votos! Uno por cada peso.

—¿Y cómo l'hizo pa la firma compadre?

—Pos jue murre fácil. ¡Primero con la derecha,
y logo con la mano izquierda!

—¿Y a qué partido le dio sus votos?

—Pos hay que ser justo, ¿qué no creye?
¡Uno jue pa los demócratas y lotro
pa los republicanos!

HAVE YOU VOTED COMPADRE?

"Have you voted compadre?"

"Why yes. Of course!"

"And how many times did you vote?"

"Well, twice."

"And how did you manage that?"

"Well, they gave me two votes."

"Two what?"

"Two votes! One for each dollar.

"And what about the signature compadre?"

"That was real easy. First I signed with
my left hand and then with my right!"

"And what party did you vote for?

"Well, one must be fair, don't you think?
"One vote went for the democrats and the
other to the republicans!"

TORTOLITA

Tortolita,
tortolita,
tus cantos
y llantos
adoloridos
punzan
mis oídos
al amanecer
sin saber
qué te duele
o te conduele.

Tu llanto zumba
y retumba
de cerro
a cerro,
de ladera
a ladera,
por todo el valle.

Cada tope
se estrella
y da un golpe
como una centella
y truenos de dolor
sin tu caluroso amor.

Tu llanto amenaza
y aprieta
como una tenaza
una grieta
de dolor
sin amor.

SWEET TURTLEDOVE

Sweet turtledove,
sweet turtledove,
your chants
and painful wails
pierce my ears
at dawn without
knowing what
ails you
or brings you pity.

Your chant zooms
and echos
from peak
to peak,
from hillside
to hillside,
throughout the
entire valley.

Each echo shatters,
gives out a bang
like a flash of
lightning and thunderclaps
of pain
devoid of your warm love.

Your chant
threatens
and squeezes
like pliers gripping
an open sore
devoid of love.

Sé que estás bien
por lo que siento
por el viento
en la sien
cuya señal
no es puñal
de dolor
sino amor.

Si me equivoco
será lo loco
que me siento
por tu llanto.

¿Por qué no te vienes
y me dices qué tienes?

Ven,
ven
a mi corral
donde un morral
cogerá
y recogerá
tu doloroso
llanto
el cual yo
ya no aguanto.

Tortolita,
Tortolita,
tu llanto
doloroso
guarda
y resguarda
mi encanto
amoroso
por ti.

I know you're well
because of what I feel
from the wind that
fans my temple.
A breeze,
T'is not a dagger
of distress
but love.

If I err
perhaps it's
the madness I feel
stemming from your lament.

Why don't you come to me
and tell me what ails you?

Come,
come,
to my corral
where a knapsack
will fetch
and secure
your agonizing
lament
which I can
no longer bear.

Sweet turtledove,
sweet turtledove,
your painful
lament
keeps
and safeguards
my loving
enchantment
for you.

EL COYOTE

El coyote ve
la luna llena
y le aulla
en el silencio
de la noche.

Sólo se oye
el murmullo
del agua
en el recodo
del desagüe
a donde
van a dar
sus aullidos
y quejidos
que se revuelven
en el descanso
de un remanso
cerquita
de mi casita.

THE COYOTE

The coyote gazes
at the full moon
and howls to it
in the silence
of the night.

All that can
be heard is
the murmuring
of water
swirling in the
river's effluvium
where the coyote's
howls and groans
land and whirl
in the comfort
of a pool of water
very near
my little house.

EL RÍO PUERCO I

El Río Puerco
se truerce
y retruerce
sinuosamente
por todo su valle,
salpicado
por un lado
y otro
de cerros,
chicos unos
grandes otros,
cuidándolo
de día y noche.

Río curioso
y misterioso.

A veces seco
otras mojado,
cuando corre
parece enojado.

Brama bravo,
con sus bolas
y olas
de agua
según va arrollando
lo que se atraviesa
por delante
de su creciente.

RÍO PUERCO I

The Río Puerco
twists
and turns
sinuously
throughout all
of the valley,
sprinkled on
one side
or the other
with peaks,
some small,
others large,
protecting it
day and night.

Strange and
mysterious river.

At times dry
while others wet,
but when it flows
it appears angry.

It bellows fiercely
with its rowdy
waves of water
as it flattens
whatever stands
in its path of
destruction.

OJO DEL PADRE*

Guadalupe
querido
con tu nombre moderno.

Ojo del Padre
el más antiguo.

Guadalupe,
rodeado de casas
de adobe,
unas grandes
y otras chicas,
pero no
descuidadas.

En el medio su iglesia,
La Virgen de Guadalupe,
a donde van a misa
doña Rosario, Elvira, y Lupe,
todos los compadres
y las demás comadres.

Guadalupe,
placita
querida
y consentida
donde me crié
y pondré mis pies
reposados
donde descansan
mis antepasados.

* nombre antiguo del pueblito nombrado en honor de un cura que descubrió un ojo u ojito (manantial) cerca de la placita.

OJO DEL PADRE*

Beloved
Guadalupe bearing
your modern name.

Ojo del Padre
the older one.

Guadalupe,
surrounded by
adobe houses,
some large
others small,
but not uncared-for.

In the center its church,
the Virgin of Guadalupe,
where Doña Rosario,
Elvira, and Lupe
attend Mass along with
all the compadres
and remaining comadres.

Guadalupe
beloved and pampered
village
where I was raised
and shall one day put
to rest my feet
where my ancestors
now rest in peace.

* the village's old name in honor of a priest who discovered a natural spring near the village which is still active today

MI CASITA

Mi casita
hecha de adobe
en la lomita
no tiene flores
ni árboles
que yo apode.

La sombra
que daba
iba
de pared
a pared,
desde la mañana
al atardecer.

Hoy mi casita
está toda solita
con sus paredes
rajadas
y cuarteadas.

Y la sombra
que queda
tiembla
y tambalea
bien delicada
con cada rendija
que la cobija.

MY LITTLE HOUSE

My little house
made of adobe
perched on a tiny hill
has neither flowers
nor trees
that I may trim.

The shadow
my little house
once formed
stretched
from wall
to wall,
from morning
till dusk.

Today my little house
stands all alone
with its walls
splintered
and cracked.

And the shadow
that remains
quivers
and wobbles
delicately
with each
enveloping crack.

EL PATITO

El patito chifla
un chiflido triste
sobre el fogón
que es mi calentón.

Su caluroso vapor
me pega de relleno
en la mera frente
cargada de un calor.

El patito siente
el pulso de mis manos
al rayar el sol levante.

Su chiflido triste
deja de resollar calor,
pues sabe que el atole*
me curará el dolor.

TINY TEA KETTLE

The tiny tea kettle whistles
a somber whistling
atop the potbelly stove
that gives me warmth.

Its gentle steam
greets me squarely
on my forehead
laden with warmth.

The tiny tea kettle feels
the pulse of my hands
as the sun dawns.

Its melancholy whistling
ceases to breathe warmth
for it knows that the blue*
corn gruel will soothe my pain.

*Harina de maíz azul hervida en agua o lecha con poca sal para dolor de estómago.

*blue corn flour that is boiled in water or milk with a little salt and then drunk for a stomach ache

EL AÑO VIEJO

Esta noche
a las doce
saca papá
su '45.

Le pone
dos cartuchos,
uno pa matar
el Año Viejo,
otro pa saludar
el Año Nuevo.

Por too
el Río Puerco
zumban
y retumban
tiros
y balazos.

¡Bum! ¡Bum!
Mi apá dispara.
El estruendo
lo estremece
de los pies
a la cara
como un trueno.

THE OLD YEAR

Tonight
at twelve o'clock
Dad takes out
his Colt 45.

He loads it
with two bullets,
one to ring out
the Old Year,
another to ring in
the New Year.

Throughout all the
Río Puerco Valley
shots
zoom
and firearms
echo.

Boom! Boom!
My father fires.
The racket
shakes him
from head
to toe
like thunderclap.

Hasta los animales
se despiertan—
las gallinas
caracaquean,
las bestias
relinchan,
mientras que
los perros
y los coyotes
compiten por
su lugar en
la confusión
de voces.

Desde San Luis
a Salazar
y de Guadalupe
al Cabezón,
con pistolas y rifles
de munición,
matar el Año Viejo
era costumbre
y tradición.

Even the animals
wake up—
the chickens cluck,
the horses whinny,
while
the dogs
and the coyotes
compete for
their own place
in the medley
of voices.

From San Luis
to Salazar
and Guadalupe
to Cabezón,
with loaded
pistols and rifles,
ringing out the Old Year
was a custom
and a tradition.

UN JONUCO

En un jonuco*
oscuro y profundo
se resbaló
un becerrito
que fue a dar
a otro mundo.

La vaca madre
brama sangre.

Jamás volverá
a ver a su hijito
a quien no conoció
sino por becerrito.

A DEEP HOLE

In a deep
black hole*
a small calf
slipped and
found itself
in another terrestrial sphere.

The mother cow
lows blood.

She will never
see the suckling
she hardly knew
except as a baby calf.

*hoyo grande de mucha profundidad

*a large hole that's extremely deep

EL CERRO CABEZÓN

El Cerro Cabezón,
padre de los gigantes
con todos sus hijos—
Los Cerros Cuates,
El Cerro de las Yeguas,
El Cerro del Chivato,
El Cerro del Cochino.

Padre no hay más fino
que el Cerro Cabezón.

CABEZÓN PEAK

Cabezón Peak,
father of the giants
with all its offspring—
The Twin Peaks,
Mares' Peak,
Billy Goat Peak,
and Hog's Peak.

There's no finer father
than Cabezón Peak.

CUANDO MUERA

Cuando muera
no me entierren
debajo de la tierra
de un camposanto.

Que desparramen
mis cenizas
alrededor de mi
casita en la lomita
donde yo me crié.

Que se las lleve
el viento a las milpas
donde yo escardé.

Que den sus
golpes y saltos
igual
que la libertad
de la cual
yo gocé.

Que lleguen
a parar
en su propio destino
sin estar enterradas
y amarradas
debajo de la tierra
sin poder volar.

WHEN I DIE

When I die,
don't bury me
beneath the earth
of a cemetery.

Have my ashes
scattered
around my little
house atop the tiny
hill where I was raised.

Let the wind carry
them to the cornfields
where I once hoed.

Let them skip
and jump freely
just like the
freedom
I once enjoyed.

Let them
rest in their
just destiny
without being buried
and glued
below the earth
without being able to fly.

EL ARADO

El arado
mancera,
cuchillo
de la tierra,
rajaba la zanja
para las sandías,
los melones, y
los chilecayotes*
que cosechaba
papá grande
entre las matas
de maíz
en las milpas
que se extendían
como una colcha
por todo el Valle
del Río Puerco.

THE PLOW

The plough handle,
knife
of the earth,
carved the furrow
for watermelons,
melons, and
chilecayotes*
that my grandpa
planted and harvested
among
corn plants
in the cornfields
that once spread
like a quilt
throughout the entire
Río Puerco Valley.

*chilecayote (chilacayote)—planta cucurbitácea que se parece a una pequeña sandía; su carne blanca (con semillas negras) se cocía en casa de mi abuelita paternal para hacer jalea del campo o mermelada. La palabra es de origen náhuatl.

*chilecayote (chilacayote)—resembles a small watermelon with black seeds; its white meat can be boiled and sugar added in making homemade jelly. The word comes from Náhuatl.

MI HERMANITO

Mi hermanito
amanece
con la jeta
colgando.

—¿Por qué estás
ahi too asolapao
haciendo pucheros?—
le pregunta mamá.

—Porque un coyote
ha matao
y se ha llevao
a mi gatito.

—Vente hijito*,
que buscaremos
otro más bonito.

MY KID BROTHER

My kid brother
wakes up
with a long
face.

"Why are you
in such bad,
pouting mood?"
asked mother.

"Because a coyote
killed my little
cat and carried
him away."

"Come *hijito**,
for we shall look
for another one
that's lots prettier."

*palabra de cariño

* a term of endearment whose closest translation is, "my dear son"

HOMBRES CRUELES

Quedó huérfano
sin culpa suya.

Hombres crueles
cuya cobardía
queda salpicada
en las vigas,
en la pared,
en el techo,
y en el cuarto
de dormir.

Con un hachazo
le rajaron la cabeza
como una sandía
donde el pobre
padre dormía.

MERCILESS MEN

He was left an orphan
though it was not his fault.

Heartless men
whose cowardice
remains splattered
on the beams,
on the wall,
on the ceiling,
and in the bedroom.

With the brutal
blow of an axe
they sliced his head
like a watermelon
where the hapless
father lay asleep.

ESPERANZA

Debajo de un sabino
descansa mi cuerpo
mientras mi alma
se sube a la cumbre
aguardando que
se resbale
la alta escalera
de buena esperanza
para poder
treparse y gozar
del bien estar
con mi Tatita Dios.

HOPE

Underneath a juniper
rests my body
while my soul
ascends to the pinnacle
where it awaits the
lofty ladder
of hope
to slide down
for my soul to climb aloft
and enjoy happiness
with my Father Almighty.

UN HUÉRFANO

Se dice que es
maldición.

Otros dicen que es
traición.

Huérfano de mente
un pobre inocente.

Quedó solito
sin padre ni madre,
arrumabado sin lugar
donde se pueda alojar.

Se la pasa rodando
por el camino
de casa en casa,
pidiendo que comer
incapaz de saber
lo que hace
y deshace.

Huérfano de mente
un pobre inocente.

AN ORPHAN

Some say it's
a curse.

Others say it's
a conspiracy.

Orphaned mind of
a poor innocent soul.

Left all alone
without father or mother,
discarded with no
place to call home.

He whiles his time away
wandering aimlessly
from house to house,
begging for food
unable to discern
right from wrong.

Orphaned mind of
a poor innocent soul.

EL HORNO

El horno
descansa solito
entre mi casa
y la caballeriza,
con el Cerro Chivato
viéndolo de reojo.

Ha llegado la Cuaresma,
también la Semana Santa
y el Jueves y Viernes Santo.

Ahora el horno echa
humo por el copete
y sonríe porque
le dan de comer
mientras él nos
devuelve pan.

THE BEEHIVE OVEN

The beehive oven
rests forlorn tucked
between my house
and the horses' shed
with the *Cerro Chivato*
looking at it on the sly.

Lent has arrived,
as have Holy Week
and Holy Thursday
and Good Friday.

Now the beehive oven
emits smoke through
its crest and smiles
because of the wood
it gets in exchange
for baking us bread.

EL RÍO PUERCO II

Hoy brama el río,
toro más bravo
no se halla.

Las olas pegan
y saltan contra
los barrancos
que escupen
terrones de agua
que se encajan
en los desagües
cornudos del
Río Puerco
como los bufidos
de un toro
embravecido.

Hoy el río brama,
toro más bravo
y terco
como el Río Puerco
no se halla.

EL RÍO PUERCO II

Today the river bellows,
a more fierce bull
cannot be found
anywhere around.

The waves splash
and bounce against
the embankments
that spew
lumps of water
that squeeze
into the horned
outlets of the
Río Puerco
like the snorting
of a raging bull.

Today the river bellows,
a more ferocious
and headstrong bull
such as the Río Puerco
can not be found
anywhere around.

DULCE DE PALITO

Hoy corren
los arroyos

por la Cañada
del Camino

con la sonrisa
de un niño

con su dulce
de palito

en la boca.

A LOLLIPOP

Today the arroyos
are running

down the *Cañada*
del Camino

with the smile
of a child

with a
lollipop

in his mouth.

CARNE SECA

La carne seca
se facetea
y tantea
de un lado a otro.

Descansa alegre
en la percha
sin granpitas.*

Las cecinas
desparejadas
parecen
chalequitos
y camisitas
colgados.

Tasajos de carne
que se orean
por la mañana
y al atardecer
mientras el sol
entra y sale.

* se usan para colgar ropa en la percha

JERKY

The jerky
shows off
and sways
to and fro.

It rests happily
on the clothesline
with no clothes pins.*

The uneven strips
of jerky
resemble
hanging
tiny vests and shirts.

Strips of beef
air out
in the morning
and at dusk
while the sun
plays hide and seek.

*used for hanging clothes on a clothesline

Camisitas y chalecos
dan aliento
al viento
que sopla
la carne
como una manopla.**

La carne seca
se menea contenta
de un lado
a otro.

Tiny shirts and vests
fan
the wind
that sways
the jerky to and fro
like a mitten.**

The jerky
swings happily
from one side
to the other.

** guante con dedo pulgar sin separaciones para el resto de los dedos.

**a glove (mitten) with a thumb but with no separate room for each remaining finger

EL OJO DE ESQUIPULA*

El Ojo** de Esquipula
sigue bullendo
su incansable agua
que refresca
el gaznate
de toda res
que baja del monte,
y el de las bestias
que suben de la cañada
a destragarse
por la tarde
después de sombrearse
debajo de los pinos
y sabinos
desparramados por
todo el campo y el valle
ardiente del Río Puerco.

*as veces escrito Esquípulas y con acento ortográfico

** ojo u ojito (el diminutivo se usaba a menudo en el Valle del Río Puerco), se refiere a un manantial cuya agua puede subir hacia al nivel de la tierra y correr; el agua que no sube al nivel de la tierra puede sacarse con un molino de viento o con una bomba de motor para el ganado.

EL OJO DE ESQUIPULA*

El Ojo** de Esquipula
continues gurgling
its tireless water
that refreshes
the throat
of every cow
that comes down from
the woods
and that
of the horses coming
up from the ravine
to quench their thirst
in the evening
after seeking shade
under the pine trees
and junipers
scattered throughout
the countryside
and scorching
Río Puerco Valley.

*at times written Esquípulas with both a written accent and an s at the end of the word

**ojo or ojito (diminutive used often in the Río Puerco Valley), refers to a natural spring whose water can rise to ground level and flow; water beneath ground level can be pumped for watering livestock using a windmill or with a motorized water pump.

LA CAFETERA

Mientras dormimos
la noche oscura
descansa la cafetera
esperando su quehacer.

Me levanto
y le echo leña
a la estufa
y prendo la lumbre
para poner la cafetera.

La tapadera
empieza a bailar
para arriba
y para abajo
del vapor
y sabor
del café que se
escapa hacia
el tabique
y el techo
de la cocina.

THE COFFEE POT

While we sleep
the dark night
the coffee pot rests
awaiting its call.

I get up
and put wood
in the stove
and light the fire
to start the coffee pot.

The lid
begins to dance
up and down
from the coffee's
steam and aroma
that rise toward
the partition
and the kitchen
ceiling.

Los cunques*
se asientan,
listo el café
para calentar
la garganta
de papá y mamá
que me esperan
acostaditos
en cama,
con mi tacita
de café y dos
bizcochitos.

The coffee
grounds* settle,
and the coffee is ready
to warm
my father's and mother's
throat
both of whom await
snuggly in bed
a cup
of coffee
and two bizcochitos.

*heces del café; palabra indígena neomexicana

*the Spanish word for coffee grounds is cunques, of Indian origin (Zuni) in New Mexico

LA PETAQUILLA

La petaquilla*
de mamá grande
guarda su mantilla
que vino de Sevilla.

La petaquilla
de mamá grande
guarda su peineta
que vino de Granada
donde el gitano canta
su lamentosa saeta
en el Sacromonte.

La petaquilla
de mamá grande
guarda muchas
cosas de herencia
y querencia
de Andalucía.

THE COFFER

My grandma's
coffer*
safeguards her mantilla
that came from Sevilla.

My grandma's
coffer safeguards
her back comb
that came from Granada
where the gypsy sings
his wailing *saeta***
at the Sacromonte.

My grandma's
coffer
safeguards many
things of patrimony
and affection
from Andalucía.

*diminutivo de *petaca*

**una triste canción religiosa que se canta en Andalucía en España durante la Semana Santa

*coffer in English, unlike its counterpart in Spanish, is not used in the diminutive

**a short and mournful religious song sung in Andalucía, Spain, during Holy Week

MIS DULCES*

Hoy día viernes
llega mi apá
del Rito de Semilla
a pasar el fin
de semana conmigo
y con mi amá.

Estoy muy contento
porque me trae
mi saquito de dulces
que compra
en la tienda
de don Ricardo
en el Cabezón.

Llega el lunes
por la mañana
y se despide mi apá.

Ya no güelve hasta
el viernes qu' entra
cuando me traidrá
otro saquito de dulces
y dolores de muelas
que pican las encías
igual que las frías
rodajas de unas espuelas.

*hechos de azúcar que se deshacen en la boca

MY CANDY*

Today Friday
my father comes home
from *El Rito de Semilla*
to spend the weekend
with my mother and me.

I'm very happy
because he brings me
my little sack of candy
that he buys at
Don Ricardo's store
in Cabezón.

Come Monday
morning
Dad bids us farewell.

He won't be back
until next Friday
when he'll bring me
another little sack
of candy and toothaches
that pierce my gums
like the cold rowels
on a spur.

*hard candy

EL CAVADOR

Todo sembrador
reclama su buen cavador.

Lo carga
al hombro izquierdo
o al hombro derecho
con gran provecho.

Con su cavador
escarda,
escarba,
riega,
y hace zoquete.*

Con su cavador
defiende su querencia
y honor.

Con su cavador
le mocha la cabeza
a las víboras
que se arrastran
por la tierra
o que andan
de pie.

*lodo; palabra de origen náhuatl

THE HOE

Every sower
boasts his good hoe.

He carries it
on his left shoulder
or on his right one
with great aplomb.

With his hoe
he hoes,
he digs,
he irrigates,
and mixes mud.*

With his hoe
he defends
his homing instinct
and his honor.

With his hoe
he chops off
the heads of snakes
that slither
on the ground
or walk
on foot.

*the corresponding word in Spanish is from Náhuatl

UN LAGARTIJO

Un lagartijo travieso
sube y baja
por el enjarre*
jugueteando
e imitando
a los viejitos
en la resolana,
unos respaldados
otros sentados,
haciendo rayitas
en la tierra
con unas jaritas
explicando
los hechos del día
del ranchero
antes que venga
y se los borre
una corriente
que vuela fría
desde el oriente.

El largartijo
se desliza
como una navaja lisa
contento de ver
y poder borrar
él mismo
los dibujos
que han dejado
dibujados
los viejitos
en la tierra.

*lodo especial hecho con paja y aplicado a la pared para proteger el adobe; origen desconocido, según Rubén Cobos.

A LIZARD

A playful lizard
goes up and down
the mud-plaster wall*
playing and imitating
little old men enjoying
the warmth of the sun,
some leaning
others sitting,
drawing lines
in the sand
with slender
little twigs explaining
the rancher's
deeds of the day
before a cold east wind
comes and wipes
their sketches away.

The lizard
slides downward
like a smooth knife,
happy to see that
he himself will be the
one to wipe clean
the doodles that
the little old men
have left sketched
in the dirt.

*special mud made with straw and applied to the wall to protect the adobe; the orgin of mud-plaster in Spanish according to Rubén Cobos is unknown.

LOS GUAJOLOTES*

Desde el chiquero
oigo a mi tía Petra gritar:

—Oye, Ocariz. Si bajas
tú con tu prima
al plan del río a nadar,
cuidao con los muchachos,
que no les . . .

(interrumpe mi prima)

—Sí, amá. Siempre
nos dices lo mesmo.

—Y si se meten
en los charcos,
cuidao con los guajolotes,
no los alborotes.

—Sí, sí, amá. Nos dijites
lo mesmo l'última vez.

—No se vaya a escabullir uno.
Ya sabes lo que le pasó
a la vaca de don Pedro,
la que tuvo cuates.

—Sí, amá, ¿pero que no jue
que bebió agua
de dos jumates**?

*renacuajos; de origen náhuatl
** palabra náhuatl

THE TADPOLES*

From the cow shed
I hear my aunt Petra holler:

"Listen, Ocariz. If you go down
to the river bottom
with your cousin to swim,
be careful with the boys,
don't let them . . ."

(my cousin interrupts)

"Yes, Mom. You always
tell us the same thing."

"And if you wade
in the puddles,
don't excite
the tadpoles."

"Yes, yes, Mom. You
told us the same thing
the last time."

"Don't let one sneak
through. You know what
happened to Don Pedro's cow,
the one that had twins."

"Yes, Mom, but wasn't it
because the cow drank water
from two dippers?"**

*the Spanish word for tadpole comes from Náhuatl
**the word for dipper in Spanish is Náhuatl

TABACO

Es martes,
los caballos
están ensillados.

Nos toca a mí
y a mi primo Demetrio
ir por el correo
a la estafeta
en la Placita.

Esta vez mercamos
tabaco de mascar
Estrella en vez
de chíquete.*

Al bajar
el río d'este lao
de la Placita,
saca Demetrio
todo ancioso su navaja
y raja
una ploga
y se lo emboca
en la boca.

(hago lo mismo yo)

Frunciendo el ceño
me dice:

—¡Hijo 'e la patada!
Éste es pura cagada.

*chicle; palabra que viene del náhuatl

TOBACCO

It is Tuesday,
the horses
are saddled.

It is my cousin
Demetrio's turn and mine
to go after the mail
at the post office
on the Placita.

This time we bought
Star chewing tobacco
instead of
chewing gum.*

As we descend
the river this side
of the Placita,
Demetrio anxiously
pulls out
his pocketknife
and slices
a plug of tobacco
and sticks it
in his mouth.

(I do the same thing)

Knitting his brow
he says to me:

"Damn!
This is pure shit."

*the Spanish word, chíquete, comes from Náhuatl

—¡No la friegues!

"Don't tell me!"

—Este tabaco
no sabe a chíquete.

"This tobacco
doesn't taste
like chewing gum."

—Dices bien.
¡Que chíquete,
ni chíquete!
Con éste nos da
chisguete.

"You're right.
This is no chewing gum
at all!
This is going to give
us the runs."

—Pus ya me tragué
el escupe.

"Why, I already
swallowed the juice."

—Y yo ya trasboco.

"And I'm about to heave."

—Ya tengo
el estógamo regüelto.

"My stomach
is already upset."

—Y el mío está
bien suelto.

"And mine is loose."

—Yo no güelvo
a mascar tabaco.

"I'm never going
to chew tobacco again."

—Es como oler sobaco.

"It reeks of armpits."

—¿Traes una tableta
de chíquete?

"Do you have a stick
of gum?"

GORGORITOS

Gorgoritos
de tierra
parpareando
en la cañada
del buen venir.

Me capean
las tucitas
aletando
sus colitas,
parada
cada una
a la entrada
de su cuna
coqueteando
como juguetes
de cuerda.

TINY BUBBLES

Tiny bubbles
in the ground
winking
in the ravine
of good fortune.

The prairie dogs
greet me
flapping their
tiny tails,
each one
standing at
the entrance
to their cradle
flirting like
wind up toys.

CONFESIÓN

—Bendecirme padre
porque he pecao.
Hace un mes que
no me confieso.
Mis pecaos son:
"Yo . . .

(me confieso)

—Hijito mío,
rézate un Ave María
y un Padre Nuestro
y vuelve cuando hagas
algo más siniestro.

(no comprendo esta palabra)

—Yo no vengo
de güena voluntá
ni con munchas ganas,
pus tamién yo
ya estoy cansao
de quebrar ventanas.

—Güeno, hijito.

—Yo vengo padre
a confesarme
porque l'Iglesia
me l'obliga.

—Güeno, anda vete,
que Dios te bendiga.

CONFESSION

Bless me Father
for I have sinned.
It's been a month
since my last confession.
My sins are:
"I . . .

(I confess)

"My dear son,
say a Hail Mary
and an Our Father
and come back when
you've committed something
more sinister."

(I don't understand this last word)

"I don't come
willingly
or gladly
since I myself
am already tired
of breaking windows."

"Okay, my dear son."

"I come Father
to confess my sins
because the Church
obligates me."

"Okay,
be on your way,
and may God bless you."

SINFOROSO

(van dos primos a pie)

—Ahi viene Sinforoso,
el joso,
ojos verdes,
cara de rabia.

—Amos echale
la zancadilla,
tú por detrás
y yo por delante.

—¿Pa, pa, pa paqué,
qué, qué, qué
hi, hi, hi, cieron
e, e, eso?

—Panqueque* lo que
comimos pal almuerzo.

—Ca, ca, ca, . . .

—Caca tú.

*pancake; anglicismo

SINFOROSO

(two cousins are afoot)

"There comes
Sinforoso,
the bear
with green eyes
and a face of fury."

"Let's trip him,
you from behind
and I from the front."

"Wha, wha, wha, why,
did, did, did,
yo, yo, you, do
tha, tha, fo, for?"

"Fortune (pancakes) cookies is what
we ate for breakfast."

"Sh, sh, sh . . ."

"Shit on you."

*the Spanish word panqueque derives from
English; hence it is deemed an Anglicism

(se ríen los dos primos)

—Bro, bro, brones.
Cabrones.

—Ámonos antes que
nos dé una pedrada.

—O nos haga
una pendejada**.

—Ba, ba, ba, bosos.
No, re, res, pe, pe,
petan a, a, naide.

(both laugh)

"Sh, sh, shi, shitheads."

"Let's go before
he hits us with a rock".

"Or he does
something stupid.*"

"Droo, droo, droo, ling idiots.
You don, don't, res, pe, pe
pect any, anyone."

**algo estúpido o insensato

**pendejada literally translates as something stupid or idiotic

EL DIENTE AJO

Me cayí,
trompecé,
y me di
en la trompa.

Me tumbé
el diente ajo,
y me quedé
molacho.

Ora espero
que salga el sol
pa que me dé otro.

—Sol, sol,
toma este diente
y dame otro
mejor qu' éste.

THE EYETOOTH

I fell,
stumbled,
and banged
my mouth.

I knocked out
my eyetooth
and was left
toothless.

Now I wait
for the sun to rise
so it can give me
another one in exchange.

"Sun, sun,
here, take this tooth
and give me another
that's better than this one."

EL VIENTO

El viento sopla
granizo de tierra
que pega contra
los vidrios
de la cocina.

Se estremecen
las puelas*
y bandejas
que están colgadas,
y rechinan
las puertas
que están atrancadas.

El viento
sopla viento
y hace unos
zumbidos
que dejan
a uno turbio
de los sentidos.

—Está como el Día
del Juicio—dice
mi abuelita
sentadita
en la cocina
con su rosario
en la mano.

*sartén (sartenes)

THE WIND

The wind blows
hail of sand
that strikes against
the kitchen
windows.

The cooking
and
frying pans*
that hang
tremble,
and the
locked doors
squeak and creak.

The wind
blows wind
and makes
humming sounds
that leave your
ears buzzing.

"It's like Judgment
Day" says my
grandma
seated
in the kitchen
with her rosary
clutched in her hands.

*the more common word in Spanish for frying pan in northern New Mexico is puela, not sartén

MI GATO

Mi gato angora
llora
lágrimas de rocío
porque tiene frío.

Quiere entrar
y estar
cobijao
al lao
del fogón,
lavándose
el bigote
pal bolote*
esta noche
de señá Senaida
y sus gatitas
en la Placita.

MY CAT

My Angora cat
sheds
tears of dew
because he's cold.

He wants to come
in and be
clothed
next
to the potbelly stove
to lick
his moustache
for tonight's
dance*
at Doña Senaida's
and her tabbies
in the Placita.

*borlote, un baile o fiesta donde hay mucho barullo

*borlote (bolote in northern New Mexico) is a rowdy dance or fiesta

LLORA, LLORA

Llora, llora
a moco tendido.

¿Quién dice
que los hombres
no derraman lágrimas?

Los que se creyen
hombrotes,
entrones,
y no llorones,
son los cobardes.

Ahi tienes a tu
tío Simón,
cara aigra
de limón,
que llora lágrimas
de niño
y de cariño.

¿Quién dice
que los hombres
no derraman lágrimas?

CRY, CRY

Cry, cry
your heart out.

Who says that
men don't
shed tears?

Those who think
of themselves as brave
hotshots
and not cry babies
are the real chickens.

There's your uncle
Simón,
who bears a bitter
face like a lemon,
but cries childlike
tears of affection.

Who says that
men don't
shed tears?

LA MILPA

La milpa
sonríe espigas
de maíz.

Cada carrera,
cargada de matas
refresca
el desierto
con sus hojas
tiernas
y verdes.

Cada mata
cargada de elotes
para tostar
sobre la estufa
o en las brasas
del fogón.

Cada elote
cargado de maíz
bien amarillo
y arropado
de cabello de ángel.

Cada elote
sonríe dientes
de alegría.

THE CORNFIELD

The cornfield
smiles tassels
of corn.

Each row
loaded with plants
freshens
the desert
with tender green
leaves.

Each plant
loaded with ears
of corn to roast
on the stove
or on the ashes
of the potbelly stove.

Each ear of corn
loaded with bright
yellow corn
and
sheltered with
angel hair.

Each ear of corn
shows its smile
of happy teeth.

¿A DÓNDE?

Las gallinas
se van
al gallinero.

Los caballos
a la caballeriza.

Los cochinos
al trochil.*

Los conejos
a la conejera.

Los potrillos
al potrero.

¿A dónde
se van la vaca,
la cabra,
y la borrega?

¿Al vaquero,
al cabrero,
y al borreguero?

¿A dónde
me voy yo?

*trox > troxil > trochil; palabra neomexicana

WHERE TO?

The chickens
go to their
chicken coop.

The horses
to their stable.

The hogs
to their pigsty.*

The rabbits
to their rabbit hutch.

The colts
to their grazing place.

Where do
the cow,
the goat,
and the sheep go?

To the cowherd,
the goatherd,
and the shepherd?

Where do
I go?

*trox>troxil>trochil for pigsty is considered New Mexican

DESPUNTAR

Despunto
y junto
lo mejor
de la mata
o lo que
se me acata.

Hago montoncitos
y pilitas
como casitas
de los indios.

Allí me escondo
en lo hondo
para descansar
en mi nuevo hogar.

¡Qué suerte tengo!
No, ¡qué suertudo* soy!

*de mucha suerte

CUTTING CORNSTALKS

I cut cornstalks
and gather
the best part
of the plant
or what dawns
best upon me.

I build tiny bunches
and little piles
like small
Indian teepees.

There I hide myself
in the part deepest
so as to rest
in my new abode.

How lucky I am!
No, boy am I lucky!*

*de mucha suerte means very lucky

EL PORVENIR

La escofina
raspa la vereda
de mi porvenir.

Que suave queda
para resbalarme
y poder volar.

Cuando yo ya llegue
a mi destino,
ni huellas quedarán.

DESTINY

The rasp
grazes the trail
of my destiny

Its smoothness
helps me slide
and hence I'm
able to fly.

By the time I reach
my destination,
no trace
of mine shall be left.

UN DESCANSO*

Muestra de muerte,
espíritu de vida,
aquí cuerpo yace,
con su alma ida.

A SHRINE*

Symbol of death,
spirit of life,
here a body lies,
whose soul sallied forth.

*hoy día en Nuevo México un descanso al lado de un camino o carretera se considera un lugar santo donde falleció un querido miembro de la familia debido a un accidente de vehículos. Un descanso suele reconocerse por un cruz de madera o metal. Algunos descansos tienen piedras u otros objetos decorativos que rodean la cruz.

*In modern times a *descanso* (resting place) is a roadside shrine marked by a wooden or metal cross to show where a loved one died in an accident. Some shrines have rocks around them as well as other decorative objects.

GRANJEA

Granjea,
gotitas de agua
y copitos de nieve
en la primavera.

Saboreo el agua
en la lengua
y la nieve
en el paladar.

Yo de niño
me preguntaba:

—¿De dónde vienen,
a dónde irán?

Hasta me sabían
a azafrán.

SLEET

Falling sleet,
droplets of water
and snowflakes
in the springtime.

I relish the rain
on my tongue
and the snow
on my palate.

I as a child
would ask myself:

Whence do they come,
where are they going?

To me they even
tasted of saffron.

DOÑA ZORRA

Anoche les cayó visita
a las señoras Gallinas.
Vino doña Zorra
a darles guerra.

Entró
por una esquina
con un gran hambre
por el alambre
de gallina.

Dejó desplumadas
a unas,
a otras
bien espantadas.

Se llevó a doña Sofía,
la que más huevos ponía.

Doña Zorra volverá,
su próxima víctima,
¿quién será?

MRS. FOX

Last night the Lady
Chickens had a guest.
Mrs. Fox came to
give them fits.

She came through
a corner of
the chicken wire
ravenous
as can be.

She left some
chickens plucked
and others
wholly terrified.

She took Mrs. Sofía
with her,
the one who
laid the most eggs.

Mrs. Fox shall return,
her next victim,
who will it be?

ZAPATOS TROCADOS

El zapato izquierdo
en el pie derecho
y el derecho
en el pie izquierdo.

Mundo trocado
y equivocado.

Lengua y cordón
por arriba.
Suela y tacón
por debajo.

Caminan juntos
mas separados.

Frente a frente
niño inocente
ve el mundo
muy diferente.

ON BACKWARDS

The left shoe
on the right foot
and the right one
on the left foot.

Confused and
mistaken world.

Tongue and shoelace
on top.
Sole and heel
underneath.

They walk side by side
but separately.

Face to face
innocent child
views the world
quite differently.

EL LAVADOR

La vislumbre
del lavador
salta de cajete*
a cajete
por el Ojo del Padre.

Día lunes de lavar
todas las mujeres
con sus quehaceres
se ponen a trabajar.

Agua hirviente,
tibia,
y fría.

Cada cajete de agua
con su
jabón,
añil,
y lejía.

Tres cajetes
forman la sinfonía.

Ropa oscura,
blanca,
y delicada,
aguardan su lavada,
enjuagada,
y secada
antes de ser rociadas
y planchadas.

¡Ay lavador
trabajador!

¿Por qué dejas
de entretenerme
con tu relumbre

*bañera o tina; de origen náhuatl

THE WASHBOARD

The glimmer
of the washboard
bounces from tin tub
to tin tub
throughout Ojo del Padre.

Monday is washday.
All the women face
their chores
and get to work.

Boiling water,
lukewarm,
and cold.

Each tin tub of water
with
soap,
bluing,
and lye
in each one.

Three washtubs
make up the symphony.

Dark clothes,
white,
and delicate,
await their washing,
rinsing,
and hanging
before being sprinkled
to be ironed.

Oh you poor hard-working
washboard!

Why do you stop
entertaining me
with your sparkle?

*cajete, meaning tin tub, was common in the Río Puerco Valley; it derives from Náhuatl

FAROLITO

¿Por qué parpareas,
farol, farolito
siendo que no está
en casa mi agüelito?

¿Será que estás triste
porque no me viste
antes de irse papá grande
de viaje al Río Grande?

Ya pronto volverá
y de seguro te traidrá
una mecha nueva
y aceite fresco.

¡Ah!¡ Por eso parpareabas
farol, farolito!

LITTLE LANTERN

Why are you blinking,
lantern, little lantern
since grandpa
isn't even at home?

Could it be that you're
sad because you didn't
get to see me
before grandpa left
on his trip to Albuquerque?

He'll be back soon
and for sure he'll bring
you a new wick
and fresh kerosene.

Aha! That's why
you were blinking
lantern, little lantern!

EL HACHA

Rita, Rita
que en el monte grita,
ni en mi casa
se queda
calladita.

Nos parte leña
muy bien engrida,
pa que mamá
nos haga comida.

Rita, Rita
que en el monte grita,
y en mi casa
siempre ocupadita.

Nos raja leños
y salpican estillas,
pa que mamá
nos eche tortillas.

Su filo, filudo
del mollejón,
lista siempre
en su rincón.

Rita, Rita,
mi güen' amiguita.

THE AXE

Rita, Rita
who shouts
in the woods,
and in my house
is never quiet
as a mouse.

She chops us wood
with great affection,
so Mom can prepare
our daily food.

Rita, Rita
who shouts
in the woods,
and in my house
she's always
busy as a bee.

She splits us logs
as splinters splatter
so Mom can stack
our tortillas on a platter.

Rita's cutting edge,
sharp from the grinding stone,
always ready to chop something down.

Rita, Rita
my very best friend.

MI PAPALOTE

Mi papalote,*
bandera en el aire
rascando las nubes
con buen donaire
para llegar al cielo.

Mi papalote,
papel de parquete
pegado con poleadas,
cruzado con jaras
del oriente
al poniente.

Me jala y jala
queriendo subir
mientras más escala.

Le doy cordón
y más cordón.

Rasguña las nubes
cuanto más sube
con su sinuosa cola
tejida en chongo
de pedazos de sábana
y baja y sube
como le da la gana.

¡Ay que alegría si yo
tamién juera papalote
pa volar bien altote!

*cometa; de origen náhuatl

MY KITE

My kite,*
a banner in the sky
scratching the clouds
with great elegance
reaching for the heavens.

My kite,
made from paper sack
glued with flour paste
from east to west
with slender twigs
in cross-like fashion.

It tugs and tugs at me
wanting to ascend
the more it scales.

I give it more
and more string.

It scratches the clouds
the higher its goes
with its wavy tail,
queue style from
pieces of bedsheet
waving up and down
as it darn well pleases.

Oh that I were also
a kite so that I could fly
way up high
into the sky!

*papalote for kite is a derivative of Náhuatl

ESPANTAJO

Soy espantajo
rey de la milpa.

Trajo sombrero de paja
y calzones pecheras.
¡Hasta pipa de elote cargo!

Soy espantajo
rey de la milpa.

Vuelan chinchontes
y también gorriones,
pero no se quedan
ni me pisotean.

El cuervo sí porque
es inteligente,
y sabe muy bien
que yo no soy gente.

¡Ay carajo
el cuervo guarda
el secreto
que soy espantajo!

SCARECROW

I am a scarecrow
king of the cornfields.

I wear a straw hat
and overalls.
Why I even sport
a corncob pipe!

I am a scarecrow
king of the cornfields.

Mockingbirds fly by
and so do sparrows,
but they don't stay
nor land on me.

The crow does
because he's keen
and knows quite well
I'm no human being.

Goodness gracious
the crow perceives
that I'm a scarecrow!

UNA LIEBRE

Liebre ligera,
que pantera
te ves
corriendo y zigzaguiando
entre chamizo y chamizo
en el desierto del encanto.

Tus brincos y saltos
sinfónicos y musicales
quedan suspendidos
en el aire con una
elegancia y finura
que apenas paletean
las espigas del zacatón
en tu gran aventura.

Liebre ligera,
se escabulle y desaparece
en las olas del horizonte
hasta el próximo espanto
en el desierto del encanto.

A JACK RABBIT

Jack rabbit fleet afoot,
you look so elegant
running and zigzagging
amidst the sagebrush
in the desert of enchantment.

Your symphonic and musical
jumps and hops
remain suspended in the air
with such elegance and finesse
that the tassels of the bunch grass
scarcely flutter
as you venture on by.

Jack rabbit fleet afoot,
sneaks away and disappears
amidst the waves in the horizon
until the next fright comes along
in the desert of enchantment.

DON ONÉSIMO

Yo soy el mero,
mero.

El gallo de todas
las pollas.

Si a alguien
le molesta,
que venga y me pique
la cresta.

Si me paro el cuello
es porque del caldo
soy el cabello.

Dirán que soy orgulloso,
y hasta poco jatancioso,
pero es que voy y vengo
porque bien me atengo
en ser un verdadero
y honesto caballero.

Si me echo el caldo
es porque SOY
el cabello del caldo.

DON ONÉSIMO

I'm the real,
the one and only lover.

The cock of the
walk.

If it bothers someone,
let him step forward.

If I put on airs
it's because I do stand
head and shoulders
over everyone.

Some will say that I'm too proud
and perhaps a bit boisterous,
but it's because I come and go
and bank on being a veritable
and honest gentleman.

If I show off
it's because I DO stand
head and shoulders
over everyone.

MI FOGONCITO

Sobre cuatro patitas
bien plantaditas,
descansa mi fogoncito
en su cuartito.

Parece un marranito
allí bien sentadito,
aún muy contento
por lo que siento.

Ha llegado el verano,
su descanso no es en vano,
me calentó en el invierno
de esos fríos del infierno.

Ahora llega el calor
que le da gusto y sabor,
sin atizarle yo la leña
cargada de una alta peña.

Que tome su larga siesta
que para él es una fiesta,
porque ya con el otoño
empieza el mismo retoño.

Vuelve mi fogoncito
a mover sus patitas,
bien plantaditas
en su mismo cuartito.

MY POTBELLY STOVE

On four tiny legs
well planted on the floor
rests my potbelly stove
in his tiny room.

He resembles a piglet
sitting down
inert but quite happy
because of what I feel.

Summertime has come,
his rest is not in vain,
he kept me warm in winter
from those hellish colds.

Now comes the heat
that gives him pleasure
and enjoyment
without my having
to poke the firewood hauled
from a rocky cliff up high.

Let him take his long siesta
that for him is like a party
for once fall comes the
same routine begins anew.

My tiny potbelly stove
begins to move his tiny legs
well planted on the floor
all alone in his petite room.

Con los leños de encino
le tengo mejor tino,
pero con un elolote
temo que se alborote.

Le abro bien el resuello
pa que se alce el cuello,
y le traiga una gran sonrisa
cada vez que expira una brisa.

Así me calienta
y tamién me alienta
mi fogoncito
en su cuartito,
durante el invierno
todo este cuerpo tierno.

Sus patitas frías
igual que las mías,
a veces tiritan del frío
rogando que entre el estío.

With evergreen oak logs
my aim is much better
but with each corncob
I fear he may get excited.

I open his flue wide open
so that he puts on airs
that bring him a great smile
each time he exhales a breeze.

That's how my potbelly
stove keeps me warm
and cheers me up in his
tiny room during the winter
when this tender body
of mine is cold.

His tiny cold legs
same size as mine
at times shiver from the cold
begging for summer to shine.

DON JUAN JOSÉ

Don Juan José se come
los frijoles con jalea
porque dice que solos
le saben a pura zalea.

Ayer estuvo en casa
de mi papá grande
mientras amasaba masa.

Entró hecho espuelas
y con sus chaparreras.

Diuna vez se arrima
y se sienta en una tarima.

Como güen vaquero
ni se quita el sombrero.

Pues dicho y hecho
le sacó gran provecho
a los frijoles revueltos
con sus cucharadas de jalea
que hasta con brel* se la sopea.

*anglicismo; pan que hacía el borreguero en el campo en el norte de Nuevo México y común todavía hoy día entre muchos viejitos.

DON JUAN JOSÉ

Don Juan eats his pinto beans
with jelly because
he claims that by themselves
they taste like sheepskin.

Yesterday he stopped by
my grandpa's house
while he kneaded dough.

He came in wearing spurs
and his cowboy chaps.

Right away he pulls up
a wooden bench and sits down.

Like a typical cowboy
he doesn't even remove his hat.

Well sure enough
he enjoyed his pinto beans
mixed with spoonsful of jelly
while even soaking it up
with sheepherder's bread.

*brel, an Anglicism, is bread the sheepherder (and cowboy) baked throughout northern New Mexico and is still common today among many old-timers

LUNA MORADA

Luna morada
en esta temporada
está de luto.

Su cara
enmascarada
en un velo
de desconsuelo
llora tristeza.

Sus cuernos
enmancornados
forman una cruz
de descanso
entre las nubes
y la neblina.

La luna morada
enmascarada
sigue de luto.

PURPLE MOON

Purple moon
the season
to be in mourning.

Her face masked
in a veil of
disenchantment
crying sadness.

Her bound horns
form a cross
of tranquility
amid the clouds
and fog.

The masked
purple moon
continues in mourning.

DON CAYETANO

La campana
de la iglesia
guarda silencio.

La gente
de la Placita
está calladita.

Ha muerto don Cayetano,
el que la campana
sonaba y doblaba
cuando misa había,
o un anciano fallecía.

Este domingo habrá misa,
pero el solo diente
no juntará a su gente
porque no hay quien
suba al campanario
y repique música
como el difunto
don Cayetano.

DON CAYETANO

The church
bell is silent.

The people
of the Placita
are quiet.

Don Cayetano
who once rang
and tolled the bell
for Mass or whenever
an old one passed away
has died.

Mass will be celebrated
this Sunday but the lone
bell will not summon
its people because there's
no one who can climb
to the clapper
to play music
as the late Don Cayetano
once did.

MOLLETES

No hay
mejor adorno
que los molletes
de mi mamá grande
en su horno.

Me arropan
y empapan
el olor
y el sabor
de la levadura
y los granitos
de anís.

Saca mamá grande
con pala
de madera,
mollete
por mollete,
cada uno
calentito,
esponjadito.

SWEET ROLLS

There's no
better adornment
than my grandma's
sweet rolls baked
in her mud oven.

The fragrance
and aroma
of the yeast
and anise
granules
envelop and
saturate me.

Grandma using
a wooden shovel
takes out
one by one
each hot,
puffy roll.

Esta noche
sin fallo
al acabarse
la Misa del Gallo
me como mis
dos molletes
que me guarda
mamá grande
en su bote de diez.

¡Qué hermosos
y sabrosos
los molletes
de mamá grande!

Tonight
without fail
as Midnight Mass
is over I'll eat
my two sweet
rolls that grandma
is saving for me
in her ten-pound can.

Grandma's
sweet
anise rolls
are
so wonderful!

AMOR

El Lolo
y la Lale
o Lale
y Lolo.

Mis dos abuelitos
bien juntitos
tupidos de amor.

Como la yerba buena
en su jardín,
no tiene comienzo
ni su fin.

LOVE

Lolo
and Lale
or Lale
and Lolo.

My two grandparents
snugly together
replete with love.

Like mint tea
in the garden,
love has no beginning
or end.

EL CALDITO*

El caldito
de mi abuelita
borbotea
suavecito
en su puela
para la cena
como los Ojitos Calientes
donde soba sus reumos.

Se guisan las papas
fritas con la carne
bien picadita
y menudita
con sus amigas
la sal y pimienta.

Ya estando guisado
hay que tener cuidado
de no comer demasiado.

No queda más caldito,
pues ya se acabó,
con brel o tortilla
cada quien lo sopeó.

*no es ni sopa ni guisado sino algo parecido a los dos; como con el caldito, ambos se hierven a fuego lento.

SOUP*

My grandma's
tasty soup
for supper
simmers gently
in her skillet,
like water at Hot Springs
where she cuddles her arthritis.

The fried potatoes
cook with
finely cut meat
and their friends
the salt and pepper.

Once ready
one must be careful
not to overeat.

There's no more
soup for it's all gone,
everyone cleaned
their plate with a tortilla
or homemade bread.

*Neither a soup nor a stew but somewhere in between; both are simmered as is true of caldito.

¿QUIERES CASARTE?

—Oye, hijito,
si quieres casarte
con güena gente
que sea decente,
vete a misa—
decía mi abuelita.

—Búscate una mujer,
no importa que sea
bonita o fea,
con tal que no queme
las tortillas o ajume
los pobres frijoles,
o lo que la plebe
hoy llama los biroles.

—Anda, vete pronto,
no seas tonto,
que ahi va Melesia
con sus dos hijas
entrando en l'iglesia.

WISH TO MARRY?

"Listen, hijito,
if you wish to marry
a good woman
who is herself decent,
go to Mass"
my grandma would say.

"Look for a woman
pretty or not as long as she
doesn't burn the tortillas
or blacken the poor beans
or what young people
nowadays call beanos.

"Come, shake a leg
don't be stupid
for there goes Melesia
(what better cupid)
with her two daughters
headed for church."

EL SOL

Cuando se asoma
el sol al levante
en la Mesa Prieta
bosteza de sueño.

Cuando suspira
el sol en la cumbre
es para despertar
a los pinos y pinabetes.

Cuando se quita
el sol la cobija
me lo capeo
con mi saguaripa*
desde mi casita.

El sol sonríe.

*sombrero de paja que se usaba cuando uno escardaba para protegerse del sol

THE SUN

When the sun
begins to peek
in the East on
the Mesa Prieta
it yawns of sleep.

When the sun sighs
at the crest it's to wake up
the pine trees
and their mates.

When the sun
removes its blanket
I wave at it with
my straw hat* from
my little house.

The sun smiles.

*a saguaripa was a straw hat that was worn when hoeing in the cornfields to protect oneself from the hot sun

EL MOLLEJÓN

Se trepa
papá grande
contoy calambres
en el mollejón.

A duras y a penas
le da cuerda
con las piernas
a la rueda
de piedra pa 'cerle
filo filudo al hacha
que está amellada*
y un poco molacha.

Chorritos de agua
del botito de hojelata
gotean en el mollejón.

A l'hacha
le da papá grande
sus güeltas
al derecho y al revés,
saltando chispas
de alegría
paquí y pallá.

*sin filo o con rotura en el hacha

SHARPENING STONE

My grandpa hops
on the sharpening stone
cramps and all.

With great difficulty
he pedals the wheel
of stone with his legs
to sharpen the axe's
blade that is dull
and a bit chipped.

Droplets of water from
the tiny tin can drip-drop
on the sharpening stone.

My grandpa turns
the axe's blade
back and forth
while sparks of joy
fly this way
and
that way.

*dull, meaning the axe has no sharp edge
or is chipped

Filuda
y templada
con el dedo pulgar,
ancha de ir al monte
por leña pal hogar,
desmonta papá grande
sin más calambres
su caballito de piedra.

Axe sharpened
and tempered,
he runs his thumb
on the cutting edge,
for it is now anxious
to head for the woods
to chop wood for our home,
and so grandpa dismounts
his stone horse
with nary a cramp.

UN BAÑO

Es día sábado,
toca bañarnos,
mañana viene gente
del Cabezón a vernos.

—¿Qué las orejas
no son tuyas?—
le dice mamá
a mi hermanito Adán.

—¿Qué quieres ir ahi
con la flor arriba
y la jedentina abajo?

(interpongo yo)

—Como la pobre Florentina,
d'allá de Santa Clara,
que ni se lava la cara
pegajosa de trementina.

—¡Pero mira cómo
me has dejao,
el cuerpo repelao,
con un' oreja coloraa
y lotra hasta moraa!

A BATH

It is Saturday,
time for our bath,
tomorrow people
from Cabezón are
coming to see us.

"Aren't these
your ears too?"
says Mom
to my brother Adán.

"Do you want to go
out looking pretty
on the outside
and all smelly
underdeath?"

(I interject)

"Like poor old Florentina,
from over in Santa Clara,
who doesn't even wash
her sticky turpentine face."

"But look how you've
left me all scraped,
with one red ear
and the other one purple.

(mamá se sonríe)

—Anda, hijito,
niña de mi ojo,
que pa mí
ahorita estás más bonito
que un piojo.

(Mom smiles)

"Come, hijito,
apple of my eye,
who for me at this
very moment is more
handsome than a louse.

MI LONCHE

Frijoles engüeltos
en una tortilla,
asina iba yo
a l'escuela
todos los días.

O papas fritas
regüeltas
con güevo,
pal lonche
o pal recreo.

No había soda
ni limonada,
con un frasquito
de pura agua,
me los tragaba.

De dulce cargaba
arroz con leche,
con pocas pasas
y su canela.

Tal era el lonche
que mi amá
me echaba,
en parquete, bote
o en una tualla.

MY LUNCH

Beans folded
in a tortilla,
that's what I
packed to school
everyday.

Or fried potatoes
scrambled with eggs
whether for lunch
or recess.

There was no
pop or lemonade,
a small jar of water
is what I drank.

For dessert
I carried rice pudding
sprinkled
with a few raisins
and cinnamon.

Such was my lunch
Mom packed for me,
in a paper sack,
tin can or wrapped
in a dish towel.

EN LA RESOLANA

—Güenos días
le dé Dios,
compadre.

—Güenos días
le dé Dios.
¿Cómo le va?

—Mire compadre,
ya nuestros
tiempos no son
los d'antes,
nos han quitao
hasta los tirantes.

—Dice bien,
compadre.

—La gente del oriente
con diente
de oro
hasta las hojelatas
nos ha quitao,
unos a pie,
otros a gatas.

—Dice bien,
compadre.

—Hasta nuestros
mesmos nietos
aquí nos tienen
abandonaos
y arrinconaos.

BASKING IN THE SUN

"May God grant
you a good morning,
compadre"

"Good morning.
How's it going?"

"Listen, compadre,
our days are no longer
those of yesteryear,
why they've even
taken away
our suspenders."

"You're right,
compadre."

"The people from
the East
with gold teeth
have even stolen
our tin plates,
some did it on foot,
others crawling."

"You're right,
compadre."

"Even our
own grandchildren
have us abandoned
stuck here in a corner."

—Dice bien,
compadre.

—Hasta güelven
de la guerra
y maldicen
nuestra tierra.

—Dice bien,
compadre.

—Ya ni hablan
mexicano,
puro americano.

—Dice bien,
compadre.

—Güeno, compadre,
ahi lo miro,
pos ya me retiro.

—Hasta mañana
sin gran demora,
si Dios quiere
a la mesma hora.

"You're right,
compadre."

"Why they even come
back from the war
and curse our own soil."

"You're right,
compadre."

"They can't even
speak Spanish,
only English."

"You're right,
compadre."

"Okay, compadre,
I'll see you later,
I must be off."

"See you tomorrow
without much delay,
God willing
at the
same hour of the day."

RESPETO

—Güenos días
le dé Dios,
compadre.
¿Cómo amaneció?

—Bien, gracias
a mi Tatita Dios.

—Oiga, compadre:

El respeto d'en hoy día
entre padres y hijos
se viene acabando.

El cariño
entre agüelitos y nietos
se viene desapareciendo.

La confianza
entre primas y primos
se está borrando.

El amor
entre padrinos y 'hijaos
se está marchitando.

RESPECT

"Good morning,
compadre.
How are you
this morning?"

"Well, thanks
be to God."

"Listen compadre:

Respect nowadays
between parents and children
is vanishing.

Affection
between grandparents
and grandchildren
is disappearing.

Trust
between cousins
is fading.

Love between
godparents
and godchildren
is withering."

—Dice bien,
compadre.

—El choque
de mano
ya se acabó.

—Es verdá,
compadre.
Ya no hay
ni caridá.

—¡Estamos bien
fregaos!

"You're absolutely right,
compadre."

"The handshake
is a thing of the past."

"It's true,
compadre.
Compassion is also
a thing of the past."

"We're really
screwed up!"

EL BAILE

—¡Qué padre*
estuvo el baile
anoche compadre!

—Bailé hasta que
se me hinchó
el cuajo.

—¡Ay carajo!

*bonito; estupendo

THE DANCE

Boy was the
dance great*
last night compadre!

I danced
till my
tongue was hanging.

Good gracious!

*padre is used idiomatically to denote
something great, beautiful or marvelous

TEPOCATES

Los tepocates,*
nuestros cuates,
protegían la cacha
de cada muchacha.

TADPOLES

The tadpoles,*
our buddies,
protected each girl's
virginity.

*renacuajos; palabra que viene del náhuatl

*tepocates for tadpoles comes from Náhuatl

EL CADILLO

—Amos
ver primo
si escardamos
después de la siesta
con la puesta
del sol.

(Llegamos
a la milpa,
y pégale un
dolor de estómago
a mi primo,
pero no traiba
*su catálago.**

No sabía
qué hacer,
si correr al escusao,
que estaba retirao,
o meterse en el zacate
*para desatar el mecate.***)

—Métete entre
el cadillo
y usa las hojas
pal fundillo—
se oyó una voz
que cortaba hierbas
con una hoz.

*catálogo Sears o Spiegel que se usaba como papel higiénico en escusaos

**cuerda; palabra de origen náhuatl

THE COCKLEBUR

"Let's see *primo*
if we can hoe
after our siesta
when the sun
begins to fade."

(We get
to the cornfield
and my cousin is hit
with a stomachache,
but he didn't have
his catalogue.*

He didn't know
what to do,
whether to run
to the outhouse,
which was far away,
or to hide in the grass
*to do his business.)***

"Hide among
the cocklebur
and use its leaves
on your butt,"
came a voice
cutting weeds
with a sickle.

*Sears or Spiegel's catalogue once used for toilet tissue in outhouses

**desatar el mecate meant to go to the bathroom

(Ahora tiene
los cachetes
bien rosaos,
igual que
*los chanates****
bien grandes
y coloraos
como dos tomates.

Rasca que rasca
con la mano izquierda,
rasca que rasca
con la mano derecha,
¿cuál de las dos
más le aprovecha?

Ha sufrido
por no haber corrido
pal escusao,
donde siquiera había
papel de parquete
*pa limpiarse l'ojete.*****)*

(Now his buttocks
have a real rash
just like his shiny red
and large balls
that look like tomatoes.

He scratches and
scratches with
his left hand, he
scratches and
scratches with
his right hand,
which of the two
is more rewarding?

He has suffered
for not having run
to the outhouse where
at least there were
brown bags with which
to wipe his butt.)

*** testículos; huevos

**** ano; fundillo

***chanates is a euphemism for testicles or balls

****butt (ojete) meaning ass or anus

CUMPLEAÑOS

En Guadalupe
los niños crecíamos,
pero años no cumplíamos.

No había velas,
candelas,
ni fósforos
para prenderlas.

Sin ningún achaque,
había fechas
de nacimiento
en fe de bautismos,
en documentos,
en camposantos,
en aniversarios,
mas no en el almanaque.

En Guadalupe
los niños crecían,
pero cumpleaños
no los tenían.

BIRTHDAYS

In Guadalupe
we grew older
but birthdays
there were none.

There were no tallow
or wax candles
or even matches
to light them.

Birth dates
without fail
appeared on
birth certificates,
documents,
cemeteries,
anniversaries,
but not on the calendar.

In Guadalupe
children grew older,
but birthdays
they had none.

CONSEJOS

—No hay mal
que por bien
no venga—me
decía papá—,
pero no te fíes
a que la suerte
venga en pues de ti.

—Ésos no son más
que sueños
que no dan de sí.

—Trabaja, trabaja,
eso sí que arriba.

Éste es el consejo
que papá me daba.

ADVICE

"There is no evil
that does not
bring some good,"
my father used
to say, "but don't
wait for luck to
come your way."

"Those are nothing
but dreams
that go nowhere.

"Work, work,
that's what makes.
you thrive.

This is the advice
my father would give to me.

CABALLO MORO

Caballo moro,
azul oscuro
d'en papá.

Desde
la sierra
al llano
la tierra
se tragaba.

Fue ligero
y atajador,
en dos patas
se paraba.

Tanto a becerros
como a vacas
apartaba,
ni a los perros
necesitaba.

Caballo moro
d'en papá,
hasta al toro
se tumbaba.

BLUISH-GRAY HORSE

My father's
bluish-gray
and dark blue horse.

From
the mountains
to the plains
he ate up
the ground.

He was fast,
and a good interceptor,
he could stop
on a dime.

He could cut
calves as well
as cows
and needed no help
from the dogs.

My father's
bluish-gray horse
could even knock
down the bull.

EL BOLILLO

El bolillo de mamá
no deja de bailar.

Con cada bola
de masa
da sus marometas
y salta una tortilla.

El bolillo de mamá
camina pa delante
y camina patrás
sin tener más oficio
que estar zas y zas.

THE ROLLING PIN

Mom's rolling pin
doesn't stop dancing.

With each given ball
of dough it performs
acrobatic stunts and
out jumps a tortilla.

Mom's rolling pin
moves backwards
and forwards
with nothing else
to do except
pop, pop a tortilla.

CHILE CARIBE

Le arden lumbre
las manos quemosas
del chile caribe
que hace con la mano.

¡Pobrecita mamá!

Cada cuantos minutos
las mete y las saca
de su ollita de cristal
llena de agua dulce
que baja del manantial.

¡Pobrecita mamá!

La punta de los dedos
le chillan y chispean
al tocar el agua,
no del susto
sino de gusto.

¡Qué alegría mamá!

DRIED-RED CHILE

Fire burns
her burning hands
from the dried chile peppers
she kneads with her hands.

My poor dear mom!

Every few minutes
she dips her hands
in her small crystal bowl
full of sugar water
that cascades from
the sweet spring waterfall
and then takes them out.

My poor dear mom!

The tips of her fingers
hiss and spark
as they touch the water,
not from fright
but from pure joy.

How wonderful, Mom!

MAMACITA

Lloro
porque te adoro.

Desde mi cuna
hasta despedirte
juites mi fortuna.

Me cuidates,
y me lidiates

Jui güeno
y tamién malcriao.

No lo hice
aldrede
sino de coraje
por ser tan maje.*

*estúpido, tonto

BELOVED MOTHER

I cry
because I idolized you.

From my cradle
until you bid me good-bye
you were my lucky charm.

You cared for me
and you put up with me.

I was a good boy
and also ill-behaved.

I didn't do it
on purpose
but in anger
for being so
dimwitted.*

*the term in Spanish is maje, which also means stupid or dumb

MIS ORACIONES

Con Dios
me acuesto,
con Dios
me levanto.

A mi santo
favorito,
el Santo Niño
de Atocha,
hasta le canto.

Tampoco
se me olvida
lo celestial.

"¿Quién en esta
casa da luz?

Jesús.

¿Quién la llena
de alegría?

María.

¿Quién la llena
de fe?

José.
Esto es todo,
por esta vez."

MY PRAYERS

With God
I go to bed
and with Him
I awaken.

I even sing
to my favorite saint
the Holy Child of Atocha.

I also don't overlook
the Holy Family.

"Who shines a light
upon this house?

Jesus.

Who fills it with
joy?

Mary.

Who fills it with
devotion?

Joseph.

That's it for now."

Glossary

The following words are common in the Hispano's lexicon of northern New Mexico; they represent a combination of influences that include Spanish archaisms, words from Náhuatl, Mexicanisms, Anglicisms, Indianisms of New Mexican origin, as well as words born in New Mexico among Hispanics (Futher information on New Mexican Spanish can be found in Rubén Cobos's, *A Dictionary of New Mexico and Southern Colorado Spanish*, Museum of New Mexico Press, 1983).

NEW MEXICAN	STANDARD	ENGLISH
A		
abandonaos	abandonados	abandoned
agüelita (o)	abuelita (o)	grandma, grandpa
ahi	ahí	there (nearby)
aigre	aire	air, wind
ajume	ahume	blacken; burn
aldrede	adrede	on purpose
amá	mamá	Mom, mother
ámonos	vámonos	let's go
amos	vamos	let's go; we go
apá	papá	Dad, father
arrinconaos	arrinconados	stuck, cornered
asolapao	solapado	bad, pouting mood
B		
bolote	borlote	rowdy dance

NEW MEXICAN	STANDARD	ENGLISH
C		
cayí	caí	I fell
cansao	cansado	tired
caridá	caridad	compassion
colora	colorada	red
coloraos	colorados	red
contoy	con todo y	together with
creye	cree	s/he believes
cruzao	cruzado	crossed
cuidao	cuidado	careful
cuidates	cuidaste	you took care of
CH		
chíquete	chicle	chewing gum
chisguete	diarrea	the runs, diarrhea
D		
de allá	d'allá	from (over) there
d'antes	de antes	of long ago
dejao	dejado	left
d'en papá	de papá	belonging to Dad
dijites	dijiste	you said, told
diuna vez	de una vez; en seguida	right away
E		
echale	echarle	to trip someone
elolote	elote	corncob
engrida	engreida	with affection
engüelto	envuelto	wrapped up
escusao	retrete	outhouse
estafeta	correos	post office
estillas	astillas	splinters
estógamo	estómago	stomach
F		
facetearse	jactarse	to put on airs
fregaos	fregados	screwed up

NEW MEXICAN	STANDARD	ENGLISH
G		
granpita	pinza	clothespin
güelve	vuelve	s/he returns
güelvo	vuelvo	I return
güen	buen	good
güen' amiguita	buena amiguita	good friend
güena (o)	buena (o)	good
güevos	huevos; testículos	testicle, balls
H		
hijo 'e	hijo de	what a, boy, wow
hojelata	hojalata	tin
I		
J		
jala	hala (halar)	pull; s/he pulls
jatancioso	jactancioso	proud
jedentina	hedentina	smell
joso	oso	bear
jue	fue	s/he went; it was
juera	fuera	were
jui	fui	I went
junta	reunión	meeting
K		
L		
'l ojete	el ojete (ano)	ass, anus, butt
lao	lado	side
l'echo	le echo	feed
l'escuela	la escuela	school
l'hacha	el hacha	axe
l'hizo	le hizo	(how) did you do?
lidiates	lidiaste	you put up with
l'iglesia	la iglesia	the church (building)
l'Iglesia	la Iglesia	the Church
llevao	llevado	taken
l'obliga	le obliga	obligates, forces
logo	luego	then

NEW MEXICAN	STANDARD	ENGLISH
lonche	almuerzo	lunch
lotro	el otro	the other
l'última	la última	the last one
M		
malcriao	malcriado	ill-behaved
marometas	maromas	somersaults
matao	matado	killed
mesma (o)	misma (o)	same
mi amá	mi mamá	my mom
molacho	sin diente(s)	toothless
moraa	morada	purple; bruised
murre	muy	very
N		
Ñ		
O		
ora	ahora	now
P		
pa	para	for
pa 'cerle	para hacerle	to make him/her
pabajo	para bajo	downward
padres y hijos	padres e hijos	fathers, sons and daughters
pal	para el	for the
pallá	para allá	that way (direction)
papalote	cometa	kite
paqué	para qué	so that
paquí	para aquí	here; this way
parquete	paquete	paper sack
parriba	para arriba	upwards
pecao	pecado	sin
pos	pues	well
prendelas	prenderlas	to light them
puelas	sartenes	frying pans; skillets
pus	pues	well

NEW MEXICAN	STANDARD	ENGLISH
Q		
quemoso	picante	hot, spicy
qu'entra	que entra	next, coming (week)
qu' es que	que es que	so they say
qu'este	que este	that man (man, etc.)
quitao	quitado	taken away
R		
regüelto	revuelto	mixed
repelado	raspado	scraped
retirao	retirado	removed, far way
rosaos	rosados	sore (from rash)
S		
sentidos	oídos	ears (inner)
subadero	sudadero	saddle blanket
T		
tamién	también	also
too	todo	all
traiba	traía	brought, would bring
trajo	llevo	to wear (clothes)
traidrá	traerá	will bring
trompa	boca	mouth
trompecé	tropecé	I stumbled
tualla	toalla	towel
U		
un'oreja	una oreja	ear (outer)
V		
verdá	verdad	truth
vites	viste	you saw
voluntá	voluntad	volition
W		
X		

NEW MEXICAN	STANDARD	ENGLISH
Y		
y 'hijaos	e (a) hijados	and godchildren
y hijos	e hijos	and sons and daughters
Z		
zigzaguiando	zigzagueando	zigzagging
zoquete	barro; lodo	mud